Million Oceans in a Single Drop

Rohini Jamwal

BLUEROSE PUBLISHERS
India | U.K.

Copyright © Rohini Jamwal 2024

All rights reserved by author. No part of this publication may be reproduced, stored in a retrieval system or transmitted in any form or by any means, electronic, mechanical, photocopying, recording or otherwise, without the prior permission of the author. Although every precaution has been taken to verify the accuracy of the information contained herein, the publisher assume no responsibility for any errors or omissions. No liability is assumed for damages that may result from the use of information contained within.

BlueRose Publishers takes no responsibility for any damages, losses, or liabilities that may arise from the use or misuse of the information, products, or services provided in this publication.

For permissions requests or inquiries regarding this publication, please contact:

BLUEROSE PUBLISHERS
www.BlueRoseONE.com
info@bluerosepublishers.com
+91 8882 898 898
+4407342408967

ISBN: 978-93-6261-125-3

Cover design: Tahira
Typesetting: Tanya Raj Upadhyay

First Edition: August 2024

ACKNOWLEDGEMENT

I express heartly gratitude to divine mother nature to make me receptive to creative insights, my family members and friends whose unshakened faith in me enable me to write and do anything else. Profound thanks to all the people who came, exist and left from my life as without good and bad experiences given by them, expressing myself in poetry would not have been possible.

PREFACE

A single emotion or expression of it has many layers underneath. million emotions we feel at the multitude of situations, few we express and many of them remain subconscious as we choose due to any reasons, not to express. Pen flitted on the rhythm of words to lay bare untold sentiments and ardour on page which led to outset of my very first book, "million oceans in single drop"

Poetry to me is just as a spiritual need which brings about me closer to self. In routine we engage in many utilitarian acts and futile too but while embroiling in art, I believe it's the time when we honestly and truly attend ourselves. Every one have their own beliefs about higher self and I seek my divine in art.

My book "million oceans in a single drop" gently and at times vehemently too, incorporates Love, sensuality, devotion, optimism, spirituality and individuality etc in a way different beads are connected in the single rosary. As a person and Being a student of psychology I believe that most of the organic diseases and psychopathology have their roots in inexpression, inacceptance and suppression of feelings because of fear of being judged or we are uncomfortable conveying. Poetry or any other artform is an acceptable medium as art entails no demarcations or judgements. Having no sacred and profanes, it is what it is.

Through this book, I want all the readers to hold my hands and dive along me in the depths of my lyrical ocean. Poetry is the vent to inner, hidden or submerged self which is crucial for sound mental health. Art has the aptness to manifest beautifully and gracefully even those feelings which may sound ugly or obscene. In this soulful journey of words, I am sure the readers will identify and associate themselves with each word and feeling of mine. Above all I am communicating with many I even don't know through my book. Embrace any form of art to feed mind and elevate soul. Give an outlet to emotions unapologetically and fearlessly.

Through my book I intend to stir the hidden string of every soul to make them hear the unheard inner music and unfelt serenity. I may not be the perfect writer but I guess successful in reaching hearts. I hope my work inspires, evokes your inner self, heals and evolves you

Finally, thanks for being besides, immerse deeply with me in the voyage to shared love, collective passion and emotions. Let me sum up my message in few words, "know yourself, work on your strengths while embracing your vulnerabilities, express your feelings dauntlessly and valiantly. It will be the highest feeling for me as a writer if my work make your 'held on tears' drop, leaves you with unladen minds and hearts.

TABLE OF CONTENTS

ACKNOWLEDGEMENT	iii
PREFACE	v
RIVER DIVINE	1
HALF OF YOU	3
NEVER SEEK HALVES	4
CHILD OF NATURE	5
ONCE AGAIN	6
LET HEART RULE	7
MY LORD SHIVA	8
I BEHOLD YOU	9
UNKNOWN SHE	10
DREAMS	11
YOU OR I	12
HOLD MY HAND	13
I PREVAIL YOU ARE THE CAUSE	15
I AM LOVE AT ALL LEVELS	16
INTERMINABLE NAP	17
LIFE	19
TO MY FATHER	20
TOGETHER, WE BOTH	21
NATURE'S CALL	22
LET ME DREAM	23

SHIVA	25
STAGNATED TO YOU	26
NOT A LIE	28
WANING MOON OF DARKEST SKY	29
THERE YOU LIE MY WORLD	30
HEALING DIVINE	31
EMBRACE ME IN REMORSELESS RAIN	32
NATURE'S REMINDER	33
THE OTHER SIDE	34
ADDICTIVE NATURE	35
MY FREE SPIRIT	36
MORE OFTEN THAN NOT	37
YOU ARE BUT MY REFLECTION	38
DEALING LIFE	39
MUST GO ON…	41
DESTINIES APART	42
ESSENCE OF LOVE OR LOVE ITSELF	43
EXIST NOT WITHOUT YOU	45
GOD MUST BE WAILING TO SEE	46
WAXES AND WANES MY HEART	47
JOURNEY OF LIFE	48
MAA	49
WANDERER OF UNIVERSE	51
ALMIGHTY, MY LORD	52
MYSTERIOUS LOVE TALE	53
EMOTIONS	55

RACE OF BLINDS	56
TRANSFORMATION	57
BEING WITH YOU	59
YOU TOO BE INSANE	60

RIVER DIVINE

wish you flow years millions River O divine,
You addicted me and did More than something does the wine
I forget all pains and good moments too
the only thing I feel and remember is you

Sun rays touch you making you shine silver white
Symbol of strength though seems pretty bold
Sun kisses you saying good bye
and you blush like Gold

Killer Queen you rule the day
what would you do at night?
No one could resist your awful sight.
You are born to charm and subdue right!

Fiercely you flow like eyes full of pride
who dies out to touch the Moon
You are certainly not that tide
who is shy and quiet. You are not even that bride

A shooter great, your arrows are straight
probably you belong to the race of cupids.
Those who embrace you might be called stupids
You hush them to sleep and sleep forever
falls prey to your charm who so ever.

Your call isn't ignorable
it fluctuates the mind as well make it stable
That holds breath, a mystic feeling you evoke
you play about with soul, it's true you provoke.

And seduce the mind like luring chant of some kind.
this pretended hush and unknown depth
must be full of mysteries and secrets you have kept
what you are up to? How you hypnotize The far I go,
the more you magnetize.

HALF OF YOU

If you are ocean, I am a drop of you
no survival as parts, single beat of two hearts
no discrete existence.
If you flame, I burn too
despite the distance
I am no one else but other half of you

O my magnificent Sun
Do you feel the fire you have?
I am someone who burns
If you are the roving Moon
craving for me in the sky I am someone within
that goes low and high

Love itself is the route and destination too
renders meaning to life and salvation too
Journey from me terminated at you
Seek me not around, I am essence within you
No one else but other half of you...

NEVER SEEK HALVES

Merge my breaths in yours
be a stranger either
touch me the way I fully bloom
or let me wither
my soul craves for intense
or nothing at all whatever dazzles
has fire so walk away if you are
frail for I never seek halves.
Sprang from the heart and
lingering on lips
awaiting to be kissed my words unvoiced
no truths to be tested no promises to keep.
Neither accomplishment or demise
till we turn to ashes
yet the love survives
Be the blow to my flames
it could be fun or defame
or walk away if you fear
for I never seek halves...

CHILD OF NATURE

Thick woods, fragrant soil
Running breeze and those rains
wish I go back to that time again
roving around trees, search for unknown
search is still on and nothing yet known
Savoring the divine, music of pines
when the wind blows
soul goes in trance and eyes overflow

Listen Mystic rivers have something to say
knowing not the destination
yet find their way with the unrivaled grace they flow
to relive those feelings, when I will chance to go!

When I will chance to roam about
those waters and mountains
when I am gonna get heavenly showers of rain
when yearning will be over to be a child again
O soils, O peaks! O rivers and waterfalls !
Every now and then you make me a call
as if someone I await, most missed and lacked
thoughts and words are hush
when the soul interacts...

ONCE AGAIN

Holding my own hand and dancing in rain
I am in love with loneliness once again
what you behold as seclusion has got
lot to say profound in its heart what you bemoan as dark
is a mystery enigmatic, the night enclasp
One more time I am diving into the solitude
deep within I am a restless ocean
O my beloved moon!
Erupting to heights, burning by your light
I want to consummate with myself once again...

LET HEART RULE

Kindles the soul, just his single gaze
compelling those eyes, met with mine in haze
single word from his lips tempts in thousand ways
A kind of hide and seek that bewitching eyes play
Touch me but within, my innermost core
You inhale my breaths, let me breathe in yours
wait a little longer till the night goes dark,
oceans turn quiet and stars too sleep
thunders go loud and clouds weep
what if unruly rain blends with wild vicious fire
before we get hemmed in conscious and desire
laying the unworldly wrongs over the worldly right
let the heart rule over the reason tonight

MY LORD SHIVA

Worldly arrows cant cleave me apart
perfidiousness of mortals, no more pierce my heart
stones pelted on me cant ripple my serenity
O feral tempest, you can't make me even dart
As I owe to you almighty
every drop of my blood
each whit of my breaths every beat of my heart
From you I emerged, in you I'll merge
with all my pros and cons, to you I belong
all my sins you sop up along my rights and wrongs
Let seraphic gleam touch me I've opened the door
O shiva I am nothing but a sprite of yours
guideless soul in a way to wild
Rebel or Misfit, but pride in being your child
I descry your might in unwavering mountains
ounce of your fire in fierce Sun,
in vehemence and spark of thunders
my magnificent lord, is your essence
Embraced all bright to dark venomous snakes you wore
whoever I am, but a child of yours…

I BEHOLD YOU

Breaths held on and eyes unblinked
with hands tight on my heart, I behold you
wondrous spell of your grace
with each sight you are new
O tranquil Moon! `each night you are new
Farther yet proximate I feel your aura to be
You drive me wild, in dreamy oceans so deep
your enchanting light enlightens soul
an esoteric bond is amid, I believe
Embosomed all pleasure
still heart feels berieved
I seek you gravely like a tide
if you come out to be a lie
I am ready to be deceived
from the world overstuffed,
yeah I need a leave
Encharmed by your serenity
and breathing your peace
eyes filled with love too with
breaths held on and eyes unblinked
darling moon, I behold you…

UNKNOWN SHE

Dreamy, bewitching, and beguiling as hell
the moment you peep in her eyes ocean deep
no escape from that prison no healing of that spell
you can be here or nowhere
who can tell flitting around the clouds dense
adrift or just lost as well
Her glance intense
Aura sedative and touch warm
those eyes irresistible, telling mystical tales
A kind of unknown unbodied charm
hard to tell when placid waters will turn to storm
Deep down the seas, yonder radiating stars
where lone she roves
Only she knows how profound,
how far under soft skin, lies a fiery heart
she lives centuries ahead of your thoughts
That tames her spirit not designed such art
mystical eyes, wink with spark divine
A spellbinding force that subdues
A mystery unrevealed, hard to find...

DREAMS

If night meant all about sleeping and no dream
whole night awake I would have been
Though I witnessed myriad sleepless ones
sleepy ones few but dreamless none
My exclusive treasure, to my core they belong
ethereal and soulfelt, an unvoiced song
inscrutable mountains, converging with the sky
Dark mysteries I explore, over thick woods I fly
scarce without you sans moon is the night
and seek you as the gloominess strives for light
Passion of youth blended with sanctity of child
what if the sublunary world be so heavenly and wild
How it feels to suspire
the scent of Angelic flowers
to descry all around beauteous and green
Real life could be more splendid than dream
If the day was so magnolious, how the night would be
and think of night so wonderous, how the dreams would be
It's indelible and Divine where goes the sight
O dream tell me where you will take my soul tonight…

YOU OR I

It was time playing puppets
healing aches, teaching lessons neither
you nor I who intends to love?
Or swerve the way overnight
let me infer not
me or you at fault
put on diverge spectacles of universe's eye
None of us were mistaken
Unwillingly reacting to nature's will
together but tracing our solitary paths
Emanating from and coaleasing into nothingness
We met to fill our voids,
destined to be depart
unknowingly performing prescribed parts
Love, sufferings, passions or whatever we interchanged
And at levels profound, the changes they brought
as if our souls were restoring balance of some sort
So rise above O love
Let's unladen our hearts
from the pains that inflicted
either you or I...

HOLD MY HAND

Darling just hold my hand
let's be wanderers of night
be heedless to the world
hear my heartbeats tonight
Let me inflame to ashes
by your hypnotic eyes
and shut my one with your lips
meeting up mine
what's just or unfair in love I know not
in your arms, I am caught
satiating my longings,
bright or dark
Now what goes right or wrong
both my body and soul
your heart is where they belong
Touch me the way
I've never been show me the crest of Ecstasy
I've have never seen
Let each bit of me
coalease to yours
Our emptiness to mingle

bodies to meet till they single
Breaths to share
I live or vanquished
I don't care
but in your arms or nowhere
Darling just hold my hand...

I PREVAIL YOU ARE THE CAUSE

Let me soar with your pace
and bathe along your flow
Your lips kissed which spell
and enchanted me, how did you?
My breaths snaveled your essence
 and I left my soul with you
Not untouched or unblemished
but a sculpture chiseled I was
You touched I suspired
Now I prevail, you are the cause...

I AM LOVE AT ALL LEVELS

That's your thing, this is mine
Darling we are different minds
All sorts together in a whole
It instantly reminds
My notion of love is a riddle to solve
and hard to define but what I feel is that
I love to be in love
All the ways, all the time
What it takes away or whatever it
yields terminate with tears or it will succeed
but my soul will never abandon to love
for love has been my survival need
Ornamented with love head to toe
No sound of it I mishear
nothing lies beyond me or lies before
dreaming or awakened
I am love at all levels
Over the wavering pride
beneath the torrent of upheavels
Yes, I am love at all levels…

INTERMINABLE NAP

Here on seeing the blazing flesh and burning bones
on the verge of river
As night turns dark, no more sighs and moans
Midnight silence is all, I can hear
Burden of Karmas, the body bears
now morphed to ashes, all good and bad
All memories I held, all possessions I had
Enjoying mellow lullaby, I'll sleep forever
may be in talks, for some longer, I'll live however
strange to see as dying embers
something I adored and loved
A body I claimed mine
created as well as perished by hands divine
Burning back to nothingness
zeroing to get a new start
Hold on your tears my loved ones
and ties of blood and heart!
Death is the truth concealed beneath life's lie
Dreams terminate with rising sun so, Why to cry?
My scent is mingling in the universal essence
soul is being purified in fire's vehemence

and will be settled on the mud
of which I was created once
the ultimate and interminable Nap
I am at perfect harmony in nature's Lap...

LIFE

It's not that you just took
there is much in my lap look!
Crucial lessons no teacher taught me ever
thick clouds burst through eyes
hiding my sun forever
But I am hell bent to keep
my promises till my final sleep
I will outlive whatever you give
Harsh and crude sides you show
will not make me bow
and devoid not me
of softness and love
hamper me, I'll outgrow
Darling life! My mysterious book
you can't keep my spirit from shine
No matter what you give
 or whatever you took...

TO MY FATHER

Breathing but not alive, somehow life will go on
as if partially functioning, all spark begone
I try to put up my broken self back
Sometimes strength also breaks
somewhere we all humans lack
and destinations too lose track I smile, I laugh and cry
that's how I carry on life
With the fighting spirit you instilled
to counter all storm and strife
With the blessings you bestowed
I'll get done all we dreamt
but the awry will be the same
These watery eyes will not see you again
No happiness will recompense this pain
Just disappeared to eyes
Or else where are you?
One thing is certain that
we all are standing in the same queue
pleasures of heaven of hell's wrath
What lies beyond the cycle of life and death
Some cord is connected, somewhere I'll meet you...

TOGETHER, WE BOTH

Whenever the night seems too dark
I'll be your light
Even if your shadow will leave
I will embrace you tight
Insane or Intense, I lessen and magnify
My love is as tender as a moon's child
Not just besides when things go smooth like somewhere, captured by storms
If life puts you off balance
I'll clasp you firm in my arms
Together we will withstand any challenge
Furious or vanquished in my shell
sometimes I can be as bad as hell
countering my hidden fights
I don't seek any word of wisdom
When I am staying quiet
Then I just need to be warm enclosed by your arms
My mood might waver
as waves go low and high…

NATURE'S CALL

The mountain peak, formidable and quiet
hark the melody ineffable
and feel inhilarting twilight
hush you O thoughts and words
let me sip you with wine
and shut my eyes till I witness divine
It's insanity or artistic lust
Laving my body and soul in the falling dusk
And I left behind myself,
all bad and good
And A void to be filled with deep dark woods
Nature utters and heals
but in subtle ways
get along with the silence
to discern what it conveys
It cries, it feels, it loves it heals
Now can't resist anymore nature's call
I have declutched myself
of affinities and all
let me wander around
thick forests and peaks
and forget everything else
to find my soul, I must loose myself...

LET ME DREAM

Do you feel my heartbeats underneath yours
drizzling in dark, incessant sky pours
and you made my eyes closed
interwining me in arms
What a flawless amalgam of serenity and storm
strangers though but not by heart and soul
who can forget the seraphic touch
of warmth and vehemence
still the body and breaths
brimming with your essence
Irresistible gaze all guards it lays
not just on the skin
he left traces of love deep within
together we seek oneness again
even if it is a sin
Dive in oceans profound
where we have never been
hold me the way, I can't escape
turn each moment into life
with no haste and waste
my words are touching you, aren't they?

Wherever you are aren't your cheeks
blushing like mine and eyes spark
who saw tomarrow for this moment,
you are mine, I deem,
shut my eyes the way you did
and let me dream...

SHIVA

Zenith of envisioning
above all felicity and pain
I witnessed you Shiva
in the frenzied fires,
in the frosting rains
the mirths I sound,
the tears I sip running as blood in my veins
where not I see you I am going insane
Quietude of Oceans
and colossal skies
profundity of the core
I descry in your eyes
Unequalled, my lord I go short of words
but my thoughts unbounded and my love infinite
no one or nothing else could sway me to such heights
O Shiva unfathomable
Almighty unrivalled
unfolding you, the Universe failed
As oceans tide up on full moon night
my emptiness and dark
striving for your light...

STAGNATED TO YOU

Benumb to step ahead,
faraway to be back
yes, I am stagnated to you
hold on to nowhere else
Knit with you so dense
as acutely twisted thread
A voice I will keep hearing in my thoughts
something will run along my veins
Core of my existence
as long as I remain
Take me to the world
distant and unknown
of love unrestrained
where I melt and you hold
Shyness surrenders and
submit to your control
your lips whispered near my ear
A tale untold
Exchanging love and heat
feeling your every beat
some words unuttered

in seducing silence
when eyes meet
I am swayed by your touch
anything working not
this way I could give up
I never thought
If I run, you do chase
if I veil, you do raise
I have fun teasing you
I would love playing games
Let me loose and you win
so my heart will let you in.

NOT A LIE

Those words of affection and mesmeric eyes
Unveiling stories untold or remorse of a kind
When laughters at once switched to sighs
As far as I recall, transient was all
But that last embrace was at least not a lie

Tears that failed to hold, pierced my soul apart
All disappeared to ashes except the meeting last
Adored we both but to extent diverge
Blazed we both but at degrees apart
All parallel and contrast, engulfed deep down
Mind awaited the separation to be accepted by heart

I end up nowhere, all that dreamt gone awry
May be here or there, like pieces fragmented somewhere
Firm in your arms, oceans I cried
From realities rasping, either escape or fight
I tasted pain of your eyes though momentary it was
But heart says not a lie...

WANING MOON OF DARKEST SKY

I am the waning moon of the darkest sky
Ceasing with each moment, far off I lie
If I meant to shatter, be it in your arms
If destined to burn, be my blazing sun

Who has attained all aspirations
Or vanquished all fights
My dreams are unalike, my tussles are but quiet
In his arms I wish to disperse
When sins of heart will eclipse the worldly right

Like a tear mingles in ocean
O lord spare me a single night
Where I end up merging in him
Stillness is all I see and hear wherever goes the sight
I am the waning moon of the darkest sky...

THERE YOU LIE MY WORLD

You are what I embody
And what is untold
And what's beyond the words
There you lie my world

The unmanifested and the obvious too
In my innocuous lies and in hidden truths
The dreams my eyes withhold
There you lie my world
Moon seeks the sun to be illuminated
Poet's imagination looks for moon to be fascinated
Each bit of us entangle and each desire enfold
Let me vanished in your arms
Dark sky, night is cold
Let's stay forever lost in our world…

HEALING DIVINE

The wind has something to warble
Night has something to say
The warmth that instantly unfreezes this pride
A tempest wild, his soulful touch can slay

Take me afar for my feet have scars
I had to dance on embers
Sometimes sing my aches
Along with lessons few more
Meet me somewhere in the way

Listen to the winds, all what they sing
And silent tales of moon untold
To behold what I see, How sun kisses moon
Mingle your senses with mine
To lose them all soon
Let's transcend the time, shed all walls of intellect
To receive healing divine...

EMBRACE ME IN REMORSELESS RAIN

I yearn not you to bring me down moon or stars
Or make me fly above the clouds so far
Just embrace me in remorseless rain
Get my wild eyes shut let me go insane

Demur not the longing of falling drops
Fleeting moments hush a bye, not to come again
Beneath unceasing sky, make most of the less
Beyond dos and don'ts too, lies a world I guess

You kiss up all my smiles, I'll kiss away your tears
Let's tune in to the silence that no one hears
Love is beyond and above human mind and heart
Spirits interwoven, seldom depart

We mortals demarcate what's wrong or right
Who knows but the breaths may stop tonight
Erelong my elation and desires go vain
Just embrace me in remorseless rain...

NATURE'S REMINDER

No matter how elevated the mountains are
When hurricanes abide by bindings
After all resisting the forces dark
How long sun can keep from shining
Clouds are meant to roar
Rains are meant to pour
Fated to be vanished, whatever embarks
In resolving her mysteries dark
Some meaning night must be finding
Prickles along the rose, can't restrain it to bloom
Can't be conquered or intimidated
Nature is gently or ruthlessly reminding...

THE OTHER SIDE

Absorbs the solitude of dark
Pain beneath the shattered clouds
For beloved's momentary sight
To be kissed by morning light
Patiently awaits whole night
as sole devotion and duty
who says moon shines graciously
just out of beauty

sometimes splintered by gales
and blazed by raging heat
meant to embrace whatever it meets
Either destined to be pierced apart
Or to be kissed by some sweetheart
With devotion profound and selflessness
What do dropped petals seek?
Gracefully scattered down to touch beloved's feet
Tell me lovely Rose, for whom your heart beats?

There's a tale behind this quiescence
Who says the Rose manifests
Just beauty and essence...

ADDICTIVE NATURE

Drained by worldly pleasures and pains I feel
Strolling in forest is all my heart needs
And somehow I get mislaid in in those woods
To haul off from the world and amalgamate with self
For I too have my phases like altering moon.
And whenever I go close and far
Trailed by something I go out seeking for
Aroma of mud, soothing wheeze of pines
As if rotating along a vicious cycle
Nature you have been always an errie
Am I after you or are you after me?

MY FREE SPIRIT

Obsessed with mountains, mud and waterfalls
Moon and stars, nature of all sorts
Driven by love boundless
Lone rover is my mind, within a nomad heart
for relentless unknown quest of soul
I need to nap in my shell and be aloof at times
 profound in inscrutable dreams
where I accept all odds and eccentricities of mine
Not the one to be carved to fit in your frame
Ask the one who endevoured
my free spirit to be tamed.

MORE OFTEN THAN NOT

No measure of how I miss you
No escape from your thoughts
Breaths mumble your name
More often than not.

Losing myself or going close to
Wherever it steers, I'll hold to
Hold my hand and come along my dream
See how infinity feels and how immensity seems

Listen to untold, descry the unseen
Together string along with moon's longest beam
Embosom me darling with no breathing space
Let the world find me till your heart they trace

Hush, O love! Let them know not
Let them ferret around and me slumber in solace
From body to spirit, let's traverse around
To reach eternity and know the unknown
Believe it or not, even if heart beats stop
Leaving breaths will somehow whisper your name
More often than not…

YOU ARE BUT MY REFLECTION

Beheld by your eyes, enfold in your arms
Turns me a bit more beautiful
Every touch of you infuses untold charm

Those moments intimate,
Even a thought makes me ablaze
My darling satiates me the way
The more I am quenched, more I crave

Liberate me from worldly knots
Hide me somewhere
Make me your essence
Where you go, take me there

Where I am accepted and loved unlimited
I am just myself, a free bird, uninhibited
Indebted to nature for this unconditional connection
I feel like talking to mirror
You are but my reflection.

DEALING LIFE

Murky gloom, I revel dealing you
Beyond the dance of doom
My arms outreaching
Above your deadliness I dare
I will embrace all stars, let the sky be clear
My moon is to shine, O night beware!
Karmic burden of bruises and wounds
Are the ornaments my soul wear all around
My forbearance will overpower
Your shower of pain
Bleeding drops of my heart
I am fond of dancing in rain.

What if life bereft me of things I desire
In mischievous hands of fate,
It feels like walking on wire
I kneel over and arise million times
Cold night you wind up
My sun will put you to fire

I hear the sighs of dropping leaves

Their dolour I can feel
Nothing I find mightier than Time's wheel
It chooses it's victims and itself it heals
Abiding laws of nature
All we can do is to stay attuned
O autumn don't laugh
My Rose is to be bloomed.

MUST GO ON...

Secrets infinite little heart holds
Probed a few, yet much untold
Cerebrating over what is done
Fretting about what's undone
In a way to one longing, dying for another
Passing moment withers charm
And the tussle makes present bother

For a moment I surmise
All that thought of is done
Think all yearnings are met
Will all miseries begone

There exists a life too beyond this unquenchable thirst
Life is serene ocean too, you just need to be immersed
soon or later, we all ascertain, in horde or alone
there is a scuffle each moment, within each one
till the final goodbye,
before the breaths cease
All hits and misses along,
life's show must go on.

DESTINIES APART

One after another, all doors seem closed
Eyes veiled by melancholia and dark
Or a venture we are acting on
Almighty once proposed.

Vision going befogged, let me illuminate my thoughts
By the beam divine within my heart
Blossom gone withered that once I planted
As life and death turned into a dream hunted
Sprinkled over all my sweat and blood
What if castle of dreams dismantled by flood.

From the earth profound to the heavens vast
No matter what we acquire but nothing lasts
When all we toil begets just vain
Lesions are but lessons of how to fight and sustain
How to handle the jouissance and be resilent in pain

Gazing the same sky yet each follows different star
Healing too is exclusive for each soul's scar
We all are born with unique
Our path's disparate, our destinies apart.

ESSENCE OF LOVE OR LOVE ITSELF

With all serenity and calm, rambling besides a lake
Anesthetic and ecstatic, only an angel could make
I kept walking on sides, with undarted eyes
Seraphic, glaring flowers were adding to the charm
All was tempting, enigmatic and luring around

Erelong I could sense or discern some harm
Stumbled around the side, with no consciousness of mind
All beauty and magic, in a flash went unkind
Before I could make out what was on
Vast and brutal the water turned
No one so far, lethal waves and me lone

Scuffling with demise, I muddled around
The more I tried, the deeper I drowned
No hope to survive, nothing worked that I tried
The frostiness of water suddenly turned warm
And I found myself laying in someone's arms

Inscrutable downright, touched soul yet unknown
Embosomed me with utmost mellowness and care
As if my pain and even breaths he shared
Some angel divine or divinity itself
Essence of love or love itself
Lying on the balance of life and death
Left in my body, just a fraction of breath
Beholding him with all haze in my sight
Somehow eyes managed to bear, the dazzling light

As if immenseness of universe merged
Shine of million suns coalesced
All woes and gloom just withered away
All undoable done in a moment's sway

Evanesced in a moment, that angel and all
Ah! Divinity and oneness of his embrace
Rest all seemed desolate and small
Going dazed in his arms
Overwhelmed with coziness and warmth

Consciousness tickled and I was lying on bed
Where was everything gone? How real it seemed !
Shook my head realizing, it was a dream
But he stirred the strings of soul or just a kind of theft
A bit of me he took, a bit of him he left.

EXIST NOT WITHOUT YOU

I do, though never meant to
Love you the way seldom supposed to
Probably a misfit in world of Ideals
But my own secluded world
Exists not without you

You were a tale untold or a memory forgotten
Followed by insight, abandoned the reason
Couldn't make how and when
But something I was surely devoid of
Unknown emptiness tingled every now and then.

Tell me if I am left alone
By the ones I claim to be my own
Will you firmly hold my hand?
Darling will you say the words, dying to be heard
Besides me will you stand?

Will you still hold on When life will show it's odds
Will you moisten my dried up lips
Bereft of breaths and words
And enfold me in your arms
And feel my unbeating heart

GOD MUST BE WAILING TO SEE

Beauty and nature all you created
All that sculptured with hands divine
No hope more crudeness to be awaited
Who knew what things turn out to be
Listen! Dried up and naked earth moans.
God you must be wailing to see

A tree whose roots sore every moment
Boughs keep breaking apart
Agony prevails as the green going pale
What worse we can do to earth's heart
Under mask of humans, demons prevail
God must be wailing to see

WAXES AND WANES MY HEART

When the day goes dim, hushing babbles of all sorts
I crave for my beloved who emerges out piercing clouds apart
Where sun's fire kneels down, your charm slays
A long way yet touches me million ways

Running ceaseless and soporific, those healing hands
Devoiding me and myself or I just entered the trance
Inflaming emotions his dazzling sight
It tickles me when the bracing breeze blows
And feel kissed when moving tresses touch my lips
Ailing emptiness is pacifying with celestial sips

I breathe in and out his love whole night
Till unenduring depart with the morning light
I call you lord of night or Mystic in dark
With your altering shapes, waxes and wanes my heart.

JOURNEY OF LIFE

Now I acknowledge a little, life is but a dream
Undecipherable script yet so vivid it seems
A journey from birth till death
How unconsciously we all, rushing to meet our ends
A frail thread bridging each breath
Getting closer to ` feared darling `
With every lapse of moment
As body and mind worn out, refining soul's wisdom
Getting unraveled with each karma `done or undone`
A tangled arithmetic of pending deeds
Sometimes reaping fruits, sometimes sowing seeds
To slumber and act out new dream again
New character to perform, a different form and name
How non- existent human existence is
And no one knows when the same will cease to be .

MAA

No recollections of when I was in your womb
What I did or used to feel, erelong I was born
No foggiest idea of how that place seemed
Still I can discern that shelter and warmth
 Raising me inside what you would feel
Indebted to you I am and always will be

Unparalled connection of soul
This bond is and ever unblended of all
Almighty I have seen you in no form,
Other than my mom
Pour her tears and pain on me
Serve her if it needs, my breaths in return
Wish to serve her my most, alive as good as burnt

Owed to you for untold things
From bearing to caring
Rendering what so ever I sought
Putting your desires on stake
To your wishes you seldom spared a thought

Your love and place couldn't be replaced

Angelic beauty and divine face
The divinity I looked at I opened my eye
Beholding the same, I wish to die.

WANDERER OF UNIVERSE

Don't mistake her winging spirit to be fickle or weak
No matter where she flies but her roots are deep
Deep down to the soil, just wayward to be reached
Chasmic as good as high, firmed as well she flies
She derives insight from sun and moon
From glittering stars, blooming flowers
And snow- covered elevations from wildwoods dark
Fierce lightning endow her with artistry
Surging rivers make her write
Give her flights of fancy the birds soaring high
In the profound solitude, her awakening lies
A wanderer of universe, alone she flies.

ALMIGHTY, MY LORD

Where the affinities have turned to the trade of emotions
To the darkest vales, we humans pertain
World goes unhinged to fit in feeble frames
To be approved or accepted in certain kind
All that exist means to be perished
Or it's just a state of mind

O where you are veiling my lord in the edges of my heart
Immerse me deep in your sanctity impenetrable
Unquiet soul will be satiated with a single drop
Make me gleam my shiva, my splendacious sun
And dissolve the dark around, with your radiance
Illuminate the doised lamps, enlighten the benighted mind
All melovolence you burn
You stay off from human senses
Beyond what mortal eyes can discern
The heart overwhelms by a single thought
No matter what what I am, virtuous or not
You run in my breaths and beat in my heart
Almighty my lord.

MYSTERIOUS LOVE TALE

And lastly he revealed the secret dark
Not a bit of inkling aforetime
That life going to be offtrack from where it was
Embraced by him, the way moon by endless sky
Yes, I was a moon, but of gloomy black night
Or some ocean cavernous, yet sere and void
For a while I thought, beyond doubts it's not,
A truth but a joke of some sort
With gaze deep, holding my hands firm
Asked me, whether or not I believe in other world
Or so called demons!
As I heard and I laughed on and on
"What came to your mind", I said
And wondered what was wrong?
"Lets follow the rhythms of heartbeats,
Lets breaths chant love all night long"
Burst somehow, with bleeding eyes he said,
Errie but I belong to the world of deads
Anyhow I dare to tell my truth dark
That's gonna rip up, I know, your frangible heart
But how could I linger on a lie

That I have no existence, I neither live or die
We have to part, destined to begone
Not to see each other from this night on
Harsh but true! Beautiful life is sometimes awry too
Let me clasp you tight one more time
Let me delve in fathomless your eyes divine
He held me like never before
That frigid night amid the seashore
You belong to deads what if so
Not by body or mind, I knew you as a soul
You know how to love deeper than mortal's hearts know
I saw no human's love so unconditional and pure
`No existence` is the ultimate end of whatever exists.
Non existence is far steadfast than the existing fake
Talk not of being depart for goodness sake
Let me merge in you though this embrace
After a moment or two, watered eyes went closed
When awake I found myself lying lone on the shore
I keep staring at the nature who witnessed those moments
Those stars, those skies
Each moment seek him, my moist eyes.

EMOTIONS

Sudden torrent of emotions
How can I handle
The castle I have been in for long
How can I dismantle
Let me know my lord
Are we humans a victim of time
Or we are under a trance
Life and death is your plan
Or purely a matter of chance
Help me clearing the clouds
To touch the piercing beam
As less I learnt, more I was taught
And grant me some toughness of yours
The same strength with which
You voided my heart.

RACE OF BLINDS

It feels strange that in the maddening world
Lonely in crowd, now warm then cold
Someone claim to be yours, you claim to be someone's
No one holds you when you are fallen once

Countless emotions you can't rely on
'Cloud of dreams' you keep flying on
Thundering leaves eyes open wide
You can't keep dreams flowing from both the sides

Hurt by those you were petted and cared
What a value of moments you ever shared!
My father, my mother, my child, my love
Numberless bonds of blood and heart
Driven by emotions, the person is caught.

Why make ties that are meant to die
Why don't we confess life itself is a lie
How long we will keep running in race of blinds
That's surely not the way to peace our soul finds.

TRANSFORMATION

And then in silence I heard, a quietly twittering birds
Unvoiced, unlyrical, yet ceaseless and mystical
As delineating some feeling earnest
To the human's soul at nature's behest

Roving alone I found departed bits of my heart
Picked up all fragments myself and put together too
After holding back and long that someone else would do
While in love I met at many other costs
A version of me unknown or somewhere lost

I saw radiating beam, while crying in dark
Illumination from within, more dazzling than thousand stars
I hail you! My pains, wounds, bruises and tears
Muddling along you I vanquished innumerous fears

Sorting the mess of my mind
 I underwent cleansing
Dealing my own chaos, propelled by life's awry
Pulled by higher meaning

Endurance is nature's art Either learnt or taught
I dealt and learnt, embraced the fire and burnt
And each moment I perished
More fortitude I earned
That's how I dealt and learnt
Lustrated every time I burnt
Blazing as gracefully as sun
Soul's transformation goes on.

BEING WITH YOU

Touching you is the most enticing art my hands find
Traces of your love can't be erased
Pleasure of oneness with you is though hard to define
Ones spent with you is life, rest is a waste

Your arms are where I wish to be imprisoned
Beyond the lives and forms
Affinity with you is something
I never felt or envisioned
With every touch of you, a bit of me transforms
With each proximation, there is more desperation
No one holds such a charm, no eyes have such seduction
Set me on fire the words, you whisper when we interweave
Slays all my shyness, like a spell they hypnotize
Your breaths tingling my skin, as a drug they narcotize.

YOU TOO BE INSANE

One more time but last
Let the longings be entwined and hearts knock fast
Come on love! Once again embrace me
and warble some unheard of song
roving in each other's skins and emotions
breathing single rhythm whole night long

Though illusion was all, your words and deeds
It was what it was, either right or wrong
Illusion but intense, futile but dense
Subsided pain to which my few aching wounds,
Dried up tears, untold fears, and at last few years belong

You wonder how I read the ashes of pages burnt
For hating the same I loved, such art I haven't learnt
Love and passion will illuminate the night dark
Both the flesh and spirit exchanging aura and warmth
Delving in ocean chasmic endeavouring to be one

From emptiness to full and full to none
Strep into my heart world through my eyes
With naked souls let's mingle again
For one more night, you too be insane.

www.ingramcontent.com/pod-product-compliance
Lightning Source LLC
LaVergne TN
LVHW061601070526
838199LV00077B/7131